REAL ID ACT OF 2005 AND ITS INTERPRETATION

REAL ID ACT OF 2005 AND ITS INTERPRETATION

MARTIN W. ARDIS
EDITOR

Nova Science Publishers, Inc.
New York

LIBRARY OF CONGRESS CATALOGING-IN-PUBLICATION DATA

REAL ID Act of 2005 and its Interpretation / Martin W. Ardis, editor.
p. cm.
Includes index.
ISBN 1-59454-724-6 (hardcover)
1. REAL ID Act of 2005 and its Interpretation. I. Ardis, Martin W.
QC173.7.T74 2004
530.14'072--dc22 2004024758

Published by Nova Science Publishers, Inc. ✢New York

CONTENTS

PREFACE

This book analyzes the major provisions of H.R. 418, which would, inter alia, (1) modify the eligibility criteria for asylum and withholding of removal; (2) limit judicial review of certain immigration decisions, (3) provide additional waiver authority over laws that might impede the expeditious construction of barriers and roads along the U.S.-Mexican border near San Diego; (4) expand the scope of terror-related activity making an alien inadmissible and deportable (removable), as well as ineligible for certain forms of relief from removal; and (5) require states to meet certain minimum security standards in order for the drivers' licenses and personal identification cards they issue to be accepted for federal purposes (a bill by Representative Tom Davis, containing only the provisions relating to drivers' licenses and personal identification cards, has also been introduced as H.R. 368, the Driver's License Security and Modernization Act). This book describes relevant current law relating to immigration and document-security matters, how H.R. 418 would alter current law if enacted, and the degree to which the bill duplicates existing law.

In: REAL ID Act of 2005 and its Interpretation ISBN 1-59454-724-6
Editor: Martin W. Ardis, pp. 1-48

IMMIGRATION: ANALYSIS OF THE MAJOR PROVISIONS OF H.R. 418, THE REAL ID ACT OF 2005*

Michael John Garcia, Margaret Mikyung Lee, Todd Tatelman

ABSTRACT

During the 108th Congress, a number of proposals related to immigration and identification-document security were introduced, some of which were considered in the context of implementing recommendations made by the National Commission on Terrorist Attacks Upon the United States (also known as the 9/11 Commission) and enacted pursuant to the Intelligence Reform and Terrorism Prevention Act of 2004 (Pub. L. 108-458). At the time that the Intelligence Reform and Terrorism Prevention Act was adopted, some congressional leaders reportedly agreed to revisit certain immigration and document-security issues in the 109th Congress that had been dropped from the final version of the act.

On January 26, 2005, Representative James Sensenbrenner introduced H.R. 418, the REAL ID Act of 2005. H.R. 418 contains a number of provisions related to immigration reform and document security that were considered during congressional deliberations on the Intelligence Reform and Terrorism Prevention Act, but which were ultimately not included in the act's final version. H.R. 418 also includes some provisions that were not considered during final deliberations over the Intelligence Reform and Terrorism Prevention Act.

---

* Excerpted from CRS Report RL32754, dated February 2, 2005.

This report analyzes the major provisions of H.R. 418, which would, *inter alia,* (1) modify the eligibility criteria for asylum and withholding of removal; (2) limit judicial review of certain immigration decisions, (3) provide additional waiver authority over laws that might impede the expeditious construction of barriers and roads along the U.S.-Mexican border near San Diego; (4) expand the scope of terror-related activity making an alien inadmissible and deportable (removable), as well as ineligible for certain forms of relief from removal; and (5) require states to meet certain minimum security standards in order for the drivers' licenses and personal identification cards they issue to be accepted for federal purposes (a bill by Representative Tom Davis, containing only the provisions relating to drivers' licenses and personal identification cards, has also been introduced as H.R. 368, the Driver's License Security and Modernization Act). This report describes relevant current law relating to immigration and document-security matters, how H.R. 418 would alter current law if enacted, and the degree to which the bill duplicates existing law. It will be updated as events require.

The 109th Congress is considering several issues carried over from the 108th Congress, including certain issues related to immigration enforcement and identification-document security. During the 108th Congress, a number of proposals were made to strengthen identification-document security and make more stringent requirements for alien admissibility and continuing presence within the United States.[1] Some of these proposals were considered in the context of implementing recommendations of the National Commission on Terrorist Attacks Upon the United States (also known as the 9/11 Commission) to improve homeland security, and were enacted pursuant to the Intelligence Reform and Terrorism Prevention Act of 2004.[2] At the time that the Intelligence Reform and Terrorism Prevention Act was enacted, some congressional leaders reportedly agreed to revisit certain immigration and document-security issues in the 109th Congress that had been dropped from the final version of the act.[3]

On January 26, 2005, Representative James Sensenbrenner introduced H.R. 418, the REAL ID Act of 2005. H.R. 418 contains a number of provisions related to immigration reform and document security that were considered during congressional deliberations on the Intelligence Reform and Terrorism Prevention Act, but which were ultimately not included in the act's final version (a bill by Representative Tom Davis, containing only the provisions of H.R. 418 relating to drivers' licenses and personal identification cards, has also been introduced as H.R. 368, the Driver's License Security and Modernization Act).[4] H.R. 418 also includes some provisions that were not considered during final deliberations over the Intelligence Reform and Terrorism Prevention Act.

This report analyzes the major provisions of H.R. 418, the REAL ID Act of 2005. It describes relevant current law relating to immigration and document-security matters, how H.R. 418 would alter current law if enacted, and the degree to which the bill duplicates existing law.

I. Preventing Terrorists from Obtaining Asylum or Withholding of Removal[5]

The 9/11 Commission Report[6] documented instances where terrorists had exploited relief for aliens in the form of asylum or withholding of removal to enter and remain in the United States.[7] Although the Antiterrorism and Effective Death Penalty Act of 1996 (AEDPA)[8] and the Illegal Immigration Reform and Immigrant Responsibility Act of 1996 (IIRIRA)[9] amended asylum procedures to reduce fraudulent claims and limited judicial review of removal orders, provisions in H.R. 418 would again amend the Immigration and Nationality Act (INA)[10] for the purpose of further diminishing the prospect of terrorists using the immigration system to their advantage.

Standards for Granting Asylum

Current Law

Section 208(b) of the INA[11] provides that the Attorney General may grant asylum to an alien who he determines is a refugee as defined in § 101(a)(42)(A) of the INA, which defines a refugee as a person who is persecuted or who has a well-founded fear of persecution because of race, religion, nationality, membership in a particular social group, or political opinion.[12] An alien who is physically present or arrives in the United States, regardless of the alien's immigration status, may apply for asylum. Although the burden of proof is not currently explicitly described in the INA, regulations at 8 C.F.R. § 208.13(a) and (b) place the burden of proof on the asylum applicant, as did previous statutory provisions.[13] Also, case law places the burden of proof on the asylum applicant.[14] The grant of asylum is discretionary and even if an applicant meets the burden of proof for asylum eligibility, asylum may be denied on discretionary grounds.

There are no explicit standards in the INA on determining the credibility of an asylum applicant and the necessity for corroborating evidence of applicant testimony. In the absence of explicit statutory guidelines, standards for determining credibility and sufficiency of evidence have evolved through the case law of the Board of Immigration Appeals (BIA) and federal courts. However, these standards are not necessarily consistent across federal appellate courts, which may yield different results in otherwise apparently similar cases.[15] An asylum adjudicator may base an adverse credibility finding on factors such as the demeanor of the applicant or witness, inconsistencies both within a given testimony and between a given testimony and other testimony and evidence (which may include country conditions, news accounts, etc.), and a lack of detail or specificity in testimony. The U.S. Court of Appeals for the Ninth Circuit (Ninth Circuit) has held that an adjudicator must make explicit the reasons for an adverse credibility finding or the court will accept the applicant's testimony as credible.[16]

Generally, an adverse credibility finding may be based in part but not solely on an applicant's failure to provide corroboration. The Ninth Circuit has held that where there is reason for an adjudicator to question the applicant's credibility and the applicant fails to provide easily obtainable corroborating evidence with no explanation for such failure, an adverse credibility finding will withstand judicial review.[17] With regard to sufficiency of the evidence, the BIA and the federal courts agree that credible testimony alone may suffice to sustain the applicant's burden of proof in some cases, but disagree on when credible testimony alone can meet the burden and when corroboration is needed. The BIA standard is that where it would be reasonable to expect corroboration, it must be provided or an explanation for failure to provide it must be given.[18] However, some circuits have criticized the BIA for failing to articulate what corroboration it expected in certain cases and why. The Ninth Circuit has adopted a standard that an applicant's credible testimony alone always suffices to sustain the burden of proof of eligibility where it is unrefuted, direct and specific.[19] One authority argues that the BIA's approach is contrary to international standards under which an asylum applicant should be given the benefit of the doubt, given the difficulties in obtaining corroborating evidence, although the applicant should try to provide any available corroborating evidence.[20] On the other hand, the U.S. Court of Appeals for the Second Circuit has asserted that the BIA standards are consistent with international standards because an applicant is supposed to try to provide corroboration for his or her claim or satisfactorily explain its absence.[21]

Currently, an alien who is inadmissible on certain terrorist grounds or who is removable for engaging or having engaged in terrorist activities is not eligible for asylum. Not foreclosed from relief is a person who is inadmissible as a member of a terrorist organization, the spouse or child of a person inadmissible on terrorist grounds, or a person who is a representative of a terrorist organization where the Attorney General has determined that there are not reasonable grounds for regarding the representative as a danger to the security of the United States.[22] As discussed below, however, changes elsewhere in H.R. 418 would much more narrowly restrict the availability of asylum to those with terrorist ties.

Changes Proposed by H.R. 418

Subsection 101(a) of H.R. 418 would amend § 208(b)(1) of the INA[23] by clarifying that the Secretary of Homeland Security and the Attorney General both have authority to grant asylum and by strengthening and codifying the standards for establishing a well-founded fear of persecution. These changes address the asylum process generally. Proposed changes that could specifically affect the eligibility for asylum of aliens associated with terrorist organizations are discussed elsewhere in this memorandum.

Authority of Secretary of Homeland Security

Although the Homeland Security Act of 2002[24] and Reorganization Plan under that act[25] provided generally for the transfer of the functions of the defunct Immigration and Naturalization Service (INS) to the Department of Homeland Security, most provisions of the INA still refer to the Attorney General and/or Commissioner of the INS. Both the Secretary of Homeland Security and the Attorney General may now exercise authority over asylum depending on the context in which asylum issues arise, and § 101(a)(1) and (2) of H.R. 418 would accordingly amend § 208(b)(1) of the INA to insert references to both the Attorney General and the Secretary of Homeland Security. However, this would only address references for that particular subsection and would not amend the rest of § 208, which would continue to refer only to the Attorney General. It is not clear whether this omission is intended to limit the authority of the Secretary with respect to changes in asylum status or procedures for considering asylum applications.

Burden of Proof and Central Reason

Subsection 101(a)(3) of H.R. 418 would codify the existing regulatory and case law standard that the burden of proof is on the asylum applicant to establish eligibility as a refugee.

However, the subsection appears to create a new standard requiring that the applicant must establish that a *central reason* for persecution was or will be race, religion, nationality, membership in a particular social group, or political opinion. Neither § 208 nor § 101(a)(42)(A) of the INA nor the relevant regulation currently refers to or defines the concept of a "central reason," which appears to be a modification of established refugee/asylum laws.

Case law concerning asylum has addressed the concept of "mixed motives" for the persecution of an alien.[26] Where there is more than one motive for persecution, a person may be granted asylum as long as *one* of the motives is a statutory ground of persecution. For example, a person may be economically persecuted, e.g., he may receive an extortion demand. If the extortion is motivated by both a desire to obtain money and by a desire to punish the person for a political opinion, or being a member of a race, religion, nationality, or particular social group, then that person may be granted asylum. However, a person may be denied asylum where economic persecution is motivated solely by the desire to obtain money rather than for the motives enumerated in the statute. The statutory establishment of a central reason standard appears to be a modification to the mixed motives standard in some case precedents.

Corroboration and Credibility

Subsection 101(a)(3) of H.R. 418 would attempt to bring some clarity and consistency to evidentiary determinations by codifying standards for sustaining the burden of proof, determining credibility of applicant testimony, and determining when corroborating evidence may be required.

Under H.R. 418, the testimony of the applicant may suffice to sustain the applicant's burden without corroboration, but only if the adjudicator determines that it is credible, persuasive and refers to specific facts demonstrating refugee status. The adjudicator may base an applicant or witness credibility determination on, among other factors, demeanor, candor, responsiveness, inherent plausibility of the account, consistency between the written and oral statements (regardless of when it was made and whether it was under oath), internal consistency of a statement, consistency of statements with the country conditions in the country from which the applicant claims asylum, and any inaccuracies or falsehoods in such statements. The adjudicator is entitled to consider credible testimony along with other evidence. If the adjudicator determines in his/her discretion that the applicant should provide corroborating evidence for otherwise credible testimony, such corroborating evidence must be provided unless the applicant does not have it or cannot get it without leaving the United States. The inability to obtain corroborating evidence does not relieve the applicant from sustaining the burden of proof.

Given the flexibility afforded the adjudicator, it is not clear that H.R. 418 would represent either a significant departure from current case law standards for credibility and corroboration or a clear resolution of inconsistencies among case precedents in different federal appellate courts and also the BIA. The proposed new § 208(b)(1)(B)(ii) of the INA appears to permit an adjudicator to make an adverse credibility finding based on the applicant's failure to provide corroborating evidence for otherwise credible testimony, unless the applicant does not have it or cannot obtain it without leaving the United States. This provision appears to be intended primarily to resolve the difference between the BIA and the Ninth Circuit with regard to credibility and sufficiency of evidence. On the other hand, the proposed new § 208(b)(1)(B)(iii) of the INA appears to be a codification of, but not a significant change from, current case law which permits an asylum adjudicator to consider factors such as demeanor, inconsistencies, and the like in making credibility determinations, as long as they are not actually speculation or conjecture, rather than factual observation.

Effective Dates

Subsection 101(c)(1) of H.R. 418 would provide that the references to the authority of the Secretary of Homeland Security would take effect as if enacted on March 1, 2003, which was the official date of transfer of immigration enforcement functions from the INS to the Department of Homeland Security under the Reorganization Plan. Subsection 101(c)(2) would provide that the asylum standards established in § 101(a)(3) of H.R. 418 shall take effect on the date of enactment and apply to asylum applications made on or after such date, therefore, the standards would not apply by statute to asylum applications filed before the date of enactment, although such standards in existing case law would apply.

Standards for Granting Withholding of Removal

Current Law

Subsection 241(b)(3) of the INA places restrictions on removal to a country where an alien's life or freedom would be threatened.[27] Although there are similarities between asylum and withholding of removal, there are also significant differences. Asylum is a discretionary form of relief, for which the standard is a "well-founded fear of persecution." Withholding of removal is mandatory relief from removal for those who can satisfy the higher standard of a "clear probability of persecution," also expressed as "more likely than not" that one would be persecuted.[28] A person who has been granted asylum has been admitted into the United States, although the status is not a right to reside permanently in the United States. A person who is granted withholding has not been granted legal entry into the United States and may be removed to his country when there is no longer any threat to his life or freedom. Withholding of removal is only specific to a particular country and therefore does not preclude removal to another country under INA § 241(b)(1)(C). An alien granted withholding of removal may not adjust to the status of a lawful permanent resident and the alien's family members are not eligible to come to the United States via the alien's status in the United States. In contrast, within numerical limits for asylee adjustments, an alien granted asylum may adjust status under § 209(b) of the INA[29] after being present in the United States for one year after the grant of asylum if the alien still meets the definition of refugee, is not firmly resettled in any other country and is otherwise admissible as an immigrant (with exemptions from certain grounds of inadmissibility). Additionally, under § 208(b)(3) of the INA the spouse and children of an alien granted asylum, if not otherwise eligible for asylum, may be granted asylum themselves if accompanying or following to join the alien.[30] Aside from the higher standard for burden of proof, withholding of removal involves similar consideration of credibility and corroboration factors[31] and some of the same issues regarding Ninth Circuit jurisprudence.[32]

INA § 241(b)(3)(A) enumerates certain classes of aliens who are ineligible for withholding of removal, including aliens reasonably believed by the Attorney General to be a danger to the security of the United States. The statute further states that an alien who is removable for engaging in terrorist activities under § 237(a)(4)(B) of the INA[33] shall be considered to be an alien with respect to whom there are reasonable grounds for regarding as a danger to the security of the United States.

Changes Proposed by H.R. 418

Subsection 101(b) of H.R. 418 would amend § 241(b)(3) of the INA[34] by applying to and codifying for withholding of removal the same standards for sustaining the applicable burden of proof[35] and for assessing credibility that would be used for asylum adjudications under § 208(b)(1)(B)(ii) and (iii) as added by H.R. 418 § 101(a)(3). The discussion above concerning specific changes with regard to central reason, credibility determinations, and corroborating evidence applies to this change as well. Proposed changes that could specifically affect the eligibility of aliens associated with terrorist organizations are discussed elsewhere in this memorandum.

H.R. 418 § 101(c)(2) would provide that the withholding of removal standards established in § 101(b) shall take effect on the date of enactment and apply to withholding applications made on or after such date; therefore, the standards would not apply by statute to applications filed before the date of enactment, although such standards in existing case law would apply.

Standards of Judicial Review for Certain Determinations

Current Law

Section 242(b)(4) of the INA limits the scope and standard for judicial review of removal orders.[36] A court of appeals can only base its decision on the administrative record on which the removal order was based; administrative findings of fact are conclusive unless any reasonable adjudicator would be compelled to conclude to the contrary; a decision that an alien is not eligible for admission to the United States is conclusive unless manifestly contrary to law; and the Attorney General's discretionary judgment whether to grant asylum is to be conclusive unless manifestly contrary to the law and an abuse of discretion. Case law also reflects these standards. The standard of judicial review for discretionary denial of an asylum claim is whether there has been an abuse of discretion. The standard of review for a denial of asylum based on a finding of fact (no persecution or well-founded fear of persecution) is whether the decision is supported by substantial evidence.[37] The standard of review for a denial of withholding of removal is whether the decision is supported by substantial evidence, since the relief is not discretionary.[38] For withholding of removal, a finding of fact that the applicant's testimony is not credible is also subject to the substantial evidence standard.

Changes Proposed by H.R. 418

H.R. 418 § 101(c) would amend § 242(b)(4) of the INA[39] by establishing standards of judicial review for reversing certain evidentiary determinations of the asylum or withholding of removal adjudicator. It would limit judicial review by barring a court from reversing the decision of the adjudicator about the availability of corroborating evidence, unless it finds that a reasonable adjudicator is compelled to conclude that such evidence is unavailable.

It is unclear whether this amendment would significantly change existing law, since the current statutory language already states that administrative findings of fact — which apparently would include a conclusion about the availability of evidence — would not be reversed unless a reasonable adjudicator would be compelled to find otherwise. It appears that this provision, together with H.R. 418 provisions establishing standards for determining credibility and use of corroborating evidence, is intended to ensure uniformity of standards for judicial review of findings of fact on availability of corroboration, although even the Ninth Circuit has held that administrative findings of fact would not be reversed unless a reasonable adjudicator would be compelled to find otherwise under § 242(b)(4) of the INA.[40]

H.R. 418 § 101(c)(3) would provide that the judicial review standards established in § 101(c) shall take effect on the date of enactment and apply to all cases in which the final administrative removal order was issued before, on, or after such date.

Judicial Review of Denials of Discretionary Relief

Current Law

Section 242(a)(2) of the INA limits judicial review of denials of discretionary relief.[41] Notwithstanding any other laws, it bars any court from jurisdiction to review any judgment granting relief under various inadmissibility waivers, cancellation of removal, voluntary departure and adjustment of status, or any other discretionary decision or action of the Attorney General regarding immigration laws for the admission and removal of aliens in the United States, other than the granting of asylum.

Changes Proposed by H.R. 418

Subsection 101(d)(1) would amend § 242(a)(2)(B) of the INA[42] by clarifying that jurisdiction is barred regardless of whether the discretionary judgment, decision, or action is made in removal proceedings. It is unclear what the effect of this provision would be, since the title of § 242 is "judicial review of orders of removal"; therefore, most matters to be reviewed would have taken place in the context of a removal proceeding. Although an affirmative asylum application may be made outside the context of a removal proceeding, such denials are not reviewable until they may be raised again in the context of a removal proceeding. In any case, the statute specifically exempts granting of asylum relief from the jurisdictional bar, whereas § 101 of H.R. 418 is intended to prevent terrorists from obtaining asylum.

H.R. 418 § 101(d)(2) would amend 242(a)(2)(B)(ii)of the INA[43] by adding a reference to the Secretary of Homeland Security, which would help clarify the text and make it consistent with the aims of the Reorganization Plan for the Department of Homeland Security.

H.R. 418 § 101(c)(4) would provide that the judicial review standards established in H.R. 418 § 101(d) shall take effect on the date of enactment and apply to all cases pending before any court on or after such date.

Repeal of the Study and Report on Terrorists and Asylum

Current Law

Section 5403 of the Intelligence Reform and Terrorism Prevention Act of 2004 provides that "the Comptroller General of the United States shall conduct a study to evaluate the extent to which weaknesses in the United States asylum system and withholding of removal system have been or could be exploited by aliens connected to, charged in connection with, or tied to terrorist activity" including the extent to which precedential court decisions may have affected the ability of the Federal Government to prove that an alien is a terrorist who should be denied asylum and/or removed.

Changes Proposed by H.R. 418

Subsection 101(f) of H.R. 418 would repeal the requirement for the study and report, apparently because the other provisions in H.R. 418 § 101 would, or at least are intended to, resolve the vulnerability of the asylum and withholding of removal systems to terrorists.

II. Waiver of Laws to Facilitate Barriers at Border[44]

Section 102 of the IIRIRA generally provides for construction and strengthening of barriers along U.S. land borders and specifically provides for 14 miles of barriers and roads along the border near San Diego, beginning at the Pacific Ocean and extending eastward. IIRIRA § 102(c) provides for a waiver of the Endangered Species Act of 1973 (ESA)[45] and the National Environmental Policy Act of 1969 (NEPA)[46] to the extent the Attorney General determines is necessary to ensure expeditious construction of barriers and roads. Despite the waiver of specific laws, construction of the San Diego area barriers has been delayed due to a dispute involving other laws.[47] California's Coastal Commission has prevented completion of the San Diego barriers on the grounds that plans to fill a canyon in order to complete it are inconsistent with the California Coastal Management Program, a state program approved pursuant to the federal Coastal Zone Management Act (CZMA).[48] The Bureau of Customs and Border Protection (CBP) within the Department of Homeland Security believed that the requirements of § 102(c) of the IIRIRA and the CZMA could not be reconciled. Consequently, legislation was proposed and considered in the 108th Congress that would have waived either a broad range of specific environmental, conservation, and cultural laws or all laws. Also, reportedly the CBP has complied with a NEPA requirement despite the waiver available to it.[49]

H.R. 418 would provide additional waiver authority over laws that might impede the expeditious construction of barriers and roads along the border. H.R. 418 would require the Secretary of Homeland Security to waive any and all laws that he determines necessary, in his sole discretion, to ensure the expeditious construction of barriers and roads under IIRIRA § 102.

Current Law

Section 102(c) of the IIRIRA provided for a waiver of the ESA and NEPA to the extent the Attorney General determines is necessary to ensure expeditious construction of barriers and roads.

Changes Proposed by H.R. 418

Section 102 of H.R. 418 would amend the current provision to require the Secretary of Homeland Security to waive any law upon determining that a waiver is necessary for the expeditious construction of the border barriers. Additionally, it would prohibit judicial review of a waiver decision or action by the Secretary and bar judicially ordered compensation or injunction or other remedy for damages alleged to result from any such decision or action.[50]

As discussed above, current statutes and the Reorganization Plan for the Department of Homeland Security have not amended and clarified references to executive authority throughout the INA. Accordingly, the reference in current law to the Attorney General would be replaced by a reference to the Secretary of Homeland Security.

III. Inadmissibility and Deportability Due to Terrorist and Terrorist-Related Activities [51]

Engaging in terror-related activity has strict consequences relative to an alien's ability to lawfully enter or remain in the United States.[52] The Immigration and Nationality Act (INA) provides that aliens at any time engaged in specified terror-related activities, or indirectly supporting them in specified ways, cannot legally enter the United States. Also, aliens at any time engaged in terrorist activities are deportable if in the U.S., but the terrorism grounds for deportation do not now extend to certain indirect support, such as representation of or membership in a terrorist organization. If implemented, H.R. 418 would, *inter alia*, (1) broaden the INA's definitions of "terrorist organization" and "engage in terrorist activity"; (2) expand the grounds for inadmissibility based on support of terror-related activity; and (3) make the terror-related grounds for deportability identical to those for inadmissibility.

Definition of "Engage in Terrorist Activity"

Under the INA, to "engage in terrorist activity" is a separate concept from terrorist activity itself. Whereas "terrorist activity" includes direct acts of violence[53] — for instance, hijacking a plane or threatening persons with bodily harm in order to compel third-party action — actions that constitute being "engage[d] in terrorist activity" include both these types of acts and other, specified acts that facilitate terrorist activity, such as preparing, funding, or providing material support for terrorist activities. Aliens who engage in terrorist activity are inadmissible and deportable.[54]

Again, and as elaborated upon below, the term "engage in terrorist activity," while including certain actions in direct support of terrorist acts or organizations, is not an essential element of all terrorism-based grounds for inadmissibility (as opposed to deportation). Distinct from support activities that amount to "engaging in terrorist activities" are actions that support terrorism more indirectly through group membership or advocacy, some of which render an alien inadmissible but, as of now, not deportable.

Current Law Defining "Engage in Terrorist Activity"

In order to "engage in terrorist activity" for purposes of the INA, an alien must either as an individual or as part of an organization:

commit or incite to commit, under circumstances indicating an intention to cause death or serious bodily injury, a terrorist activity;

prepare or plan a terrorist activity;

gather information on potential targets for a terrorist activity;

solicit funds or other things of value for a terrorist activity or terrorist organization;

solicit another individual to engage in terrorist activity or join a terrorist organization; or

commit an act that the alien knows, or reasonably should know, provides material support — including a safe house, transportation, communications, funds, transfer of funds or other material financial benefit, false documentation or identification, weapons (including chemical, biological, or radiological weapons), explosives, or training — to an individual or organization that the alien knows or should reasonably know has committed or plans to commit a terrorist activity.[55]

With respect to acts related to a "terrorist organization," acts through or on behalf of an organization formally designated by the Government as terrorist are covered regardless of an individual's knowledge of the organization's terrorist connections. However, if an alien has acted as a solicitor or provided material support for an organization that has not been formally designated as a terrorist organization by the United States, but which has nevertheless committed, incited, planned, prepared, or gathered information for a terrorist activity, the alien may be deemed not to have engaged in terrorist activity himself if he can demonstrate that he did not and should not have reasonably known that his solicitation or material support would further the organization's terrorist activities.[56]

Under present law, the material support clause within the INA's definition of "engage in terrorist activity" may be waived in application to a specific alien if the Secretary of State, after consultation with the Attorney General, or the Attorney General, after consultation with the Secretary of State, concludes in his sole unreviewable discretion that this clause should not apply.[57]

Changes Proposed by H.R. 418 to the Definition of "Engage in Terrorist Activity"

Section 103(b) of H.R. 418 would replace the current definition of "engage in terrorist activity" found in INA § 212(a)(3)(B)(iv) with a new definition. For the most part, this definition would be identical to the previous version. However, a few significant changes would also be made.

More Stringent Provisions Relating to Material Support, Solicitation of Funds or Participation in Non-designated Terrorist Organizations/Activities

H.R. 418 would make it more difficult for an alien who has provided material support or acted as a solicitor for either a person engaged in terrorist activity or a non-designated terrorist organization to avoid being found to have engaged in terrorist activity himself. Under present law, an alien may avoid being found to have engaged in terrorist activity if he can demonstrate that he did not and should not have reasonably known that his solicitation or material support to an individual or non-designated terrorist organization would further terrorist activities.[58] Pursuant to the amendments proposed by H.R. 418 § 103(b), an alien would have to demonstrate *by clear and convincing evidence* (a higher standard) that he did not and should not have reasonably known that his solicitation or material support would further a terrorist activity or organization in order to be found not to have engaged in terrorist activity himself.[59]

Removes Authority to Waive Material Support Provision

H.R. 418 removes the authority of the Secretary of State and Attorney General to waive application of the material support clause within the INA's definition of "engage in terrorist activity."

Effective Date of Proposed Changes to the Definition of "Engage in Terrorist Activity"

Pursuant to § 103(c) of H.R. 418, the proposed changes to the INA's definition of "engage in terrorist activity" would be effective on the date of H.R. 418's enactment, and apply to removal proceedings instituted before or after H.R. 418's enactment, as well as to acts and conditions constituting a ground for inadmissibility occurring or existing before or after H.R. 418's enactment.

Definition of "Terrorist Organization"

The INA defines "terrorist organization" to include both groups designated as such by the Secretary of State and non-designated groups that engage in specified terror-related activities.[60] Certain forms of assistance to a "terrorist organization"are grounds for inadmissibility and deportability because they amount to "engaging in a terrorist activity". Furthermore, under current law, certain memberships in or associations with a "terrorist organization" may be grounds for inadmissibility even though such membership or association, *vel non*, may not make an alien deportable.[61] Accordingly, amending the definition of "terrorist organization" might have a considerable impact on the reach of other terrorism-related provisions of the INA.

Current Law Defining "Terrorist Organization"

INA § 212(a)(3)(B)(vi) presently defines "terrorist organization" as including:

any group designated by the Secretary of State as a terrorist organization pursuant to INA § 219;[62]

upon publication in the Federal Register, any group designated as a terrorist organization by the Secretary of State in consultation with or upon the request of the Attorney General, after finding that the organization commits, incites, plans, prepares, gathers information, or provides material support for terrorist activities; or

a group of two or more individuals, whether organized or not, which commits, incites, plans, prepares, or gathers information for terrorist activities.[63]

Changes Proposed by H.R. 418

Section 103(c) of H.R. 418 amends the current definition of "terrorist organization" found in INA § 212(a)(3)(B)(vi). The proposed amendments, discussed below, are significant and, in combination with the proposed expansion of the types of associations with a terrorist organization that can lead to an alien's inadmissibility/deportation, may greatly amplify the reach of the terrorism provisions of the INA generally. Among other contexts, the proposed changes could especially impact aliens associated with groups that are part of a web of fund raising that is found to support a terrorist activity in some measure.

Retention of Attorney General's Role in the Designation of Terrorist Organizations

Most of the authority to administer immigration law that formerly was held by the Attorney General has been transferred to the Secretary of Homeland Security, though some authorities have been retained. Section 103(c) of H.R. 418 would provide both the Secretary of Homeland Security and the Attorney General with an express role in the designation of groups as terrorist organizations that are not otherwise designated as such by the Secretary of State pursuant to INA § 219. H.R. 418 would amend the INA's definition of "terrorist organization" to include any group designated as such by the Secretary of State, in consultation with or upon the request of the Attorney General *or* the Secretary of Homeland Security, to designate a group as a terrorist organization after finding that the organization "engages in terrorist activity," as defined under INA § 212(a)(3)(B)(iv).

Expanding the Activities Qualifying a Non-designated Group as a Terrorist Organization

H.R. 418's proposed amendment to the INA's definition of "terrorist organization" could significantly increase the number of groups that would constitute terrorist organizations despite not being designated as such by the Secretary of State.

First, under current law, a group not otherwise designated by the Secretary of State can only be deemed a terrorist organization if the group commits, incites, plans, prepares, or gathers information for terrorist activity.[64] Under H.R. 418, a group not otherwise designated as a terrorist organization could also be considered such if it solicits funds or membership for a terrorist activity or terrorist organization or otherwise provides material support for a terrorist activity or organization. The reach of this extension may not be altogether clear: it appears uncertain as to whether or how a group could escape coverage by showing that it could not reasonably have known that an organization for which it solicited or provided material support was itself involved in conducting terrorist acts or supporting a "terrorist organization," (as redefined), and so on down the chain.

Second, H.R. 418 § 103(c) would further amend "terrorist organization" to include any non-designated group that has a subgroup that "engages in terrorist activity," as expanded by H.R. 418 in this context to include either (1) direct participation in or support of a terrorist activity or organization, or (2) indirect support through solicitation, recruitment, etc. The upshot of the inclusion of subgroups may be to further lower the threshold for how substantial, apparent, and immediate a group's support must be for a terrorist activity or organization for the group to be considered "terrorist" and for its members to potentially fall within the terrorism provisions of the INA. For example, if organization A has a subgroup A1 that raises funds for organization B (among other groups) and organization B distributes funds to organization C (among other groups), which has a subgroup C1 that at some point provided support to a terrorist activity or organization, organization A apparently would qualify as a terrorist organization (and its member fall under the grounds of inadmissibility/deportability discussed below) absent the group's ability to somehow extricate itself by showing it could not have reasonably drawn the connection between its subgroup's fund raising and subgroup C1.

Effective Date of Proposed Changes to the Definition of "Terrorist Organization"

Pursuant to § 103(c) of H.R. 418, the proposed changes to the INA's definition of "terrorist organization" would be effective on the date of H.R. 418's enactment, and apply to removal proceedings instituted before or after H.R. 418's enactment, as well as to acts and conditions constituting a ground for inadmissibility occurring or existing before or after H.R. 418's enactment.

Terror-Related Grounds for Inadmissibility of Aliens

The INA categorizes certain classes of aliens as inadmissible, making them "ineligible to receive visas and ineligible to be admitted to the United States."[65] Aliens who "engage in terrorist activity," as defined by INA § 212(a)(3)(B)(iv), are inadmissible. In addition, several other terror-related activities are grounds for inadmissibility.

Current Law

Pursuant to INA § 212(a)(3)(B)(i),[66] an alien is inadmissible on terror-related grounds if the alien:

has engaged in terrorist activity; CRS-17 [67] The limited exception to inadmissibility for the spouse and child of an alien who is inadmissible on terror-related grounds is found in INA § 212(a)(3)(B)(ii).

is known or reasonably believed by a consular officer or the Attorney General to be engaged in or likely to engage in terrorist activity upon entry into the United States;

has, under circumstances indicating an intention to cause death or serious bodily harm, incited terrorist activity;

is a representative of (1) a foreign terrorist organization, as designated by the Secretary of State, or (2) a political, social or other similar group whose public endorsement of acts of terrorist activity the Secretary of State has determined undermines United States efforts to reduce or eliminate terrorist activities;

is a member of a foreign terrorist organization as designated by the Secretary of State under INA § 219, or an organization which the alien knows or should have known is a terrorist organization;

is an officer, official, representative, or spokesman of the Palestine Liberation Organization;

has used his position of prominence within any country to endorse or espouse terrorist activity, or to persuade others to support terrorist activity or a terrorist organization, in a way that the Secretary of State has determined undermines United States efforts to reduce or eliminate terrorist activities; or

is the spouse or child of an alien who is inadmissible under this section, if the activity causing the alien to be found inadmissible occurred within the last five years, *unless* the spouse or child (1) did not and should not have reasonably known about the terrorist activity or (2) in the reasonable belief of the consular officer or Attorney General, has renounced the activity causing the alien to be found inadmissible under this section.67

In addition, INA § 212(a)(3)(F) designates an alien as inadmissible if the Secretary of State, after consultation with the Attorney General, or the Attorney General, after consultation with the Secretary of State, determines that the alien has been associated with a terrorist organization and intends while in the United States to engage solely, principally, or incidentally in activities that could endanger the welfare, safety, or security of the United States.

Changes to Terror-Related Grounds for Inadmissibility Proposed by H.R. 418

Section 103(a) of H.R. 418 would reorganize and expand the terror-related grounds for inadmissibility. Given that H.R. 418 § 103(b)-(c) would broaden the INA's definitions of "terrorist organization" and "engage in terrorist activity" — two phrases frequently used in the INA provisions establishing the terror-related grounds for inadmissibility — H.R. 418 would expand the terror-related grounds for inadmissibility more broadly than might first appear. The interplay between the proposed definition of "terrorist organization," discussed above, and the expansion of covered support and associational activities, discussed below, may be particularly significant in broadening the grounds for inadmissibility.

The following paragraphs discuss the alterations that H.R. 418 would make to the terror-related grounds for inadmissibility.

Effects of Expanded Definition of "Engage in Terrorist Activity" on Terror-Related Grounds for Inadmissibility

As in current law, H.R. 418 provides that any alien who has engaged in a terrorist activity is inadmissible.[68] As previously mentioned, § 103(b) of H.R. 418 would expand the applicable definition of the term "engage in terrorist activity." Thus, under H.R. 418, an alien who solicited on behalf of or provided material support for a non-designated terrorist organization would be inadmissible unless he demonstrated *by clear and convincing evidence* that he did not and should not have reasonably known that he was soliciting on behalf of or providing material support for a group that met the definition of "terrorist organization" found in INA § 212(a)(3)(B)(vi)(III).

Retention of Attorney General's Role in Deeming an Alien Inadmissible for Terror-Related Activity

Though recent law has transferred most immigration enforcement authority to the Department of Homeland Security, H.R. 418 would allow a consular officer, the Secretary of Homeland Security, or the Attorney General to declare an alien inadmissible if the alien is known to be engaged in terrorist activity or is likely to engage in such activity upon entry into the United States.[69]

Incitement of Terrorist Activity

H.R. 418 does not alter the current ground for inadmissibility on account of the incitement of terrorist activity.

Representation of a Terrorist Organization or Political Group Espousing Terrorist Activity

Under current law, a representative of a foreign terrorist organization designated as such by the Secretary of State is inadmissible. H.R. 418 would expand this ground for inadmissibility to deny admission to a representative of *any* group that constituted a "terrorist organization," as defined under INA § 212(a)(3)(B)(vi). As previously discussed, H.R. 418 would expand the breadth of the term "terrorist organization" for purposes of the INA. H.R.

418 would also make inadmissible *any* representative of a political, social or other similar group that endorses or espouses terrorist activity.[70] Under current law, such representatives are only inadmissible if (1) the organization *publicly endorses* terrorist activity and (2) the Secretary of State determines that such endorsement undermines U.S. efforts to reduce or eliminate terrorist activities.[71]

Membership in a Terrorist Organization

H.R. 418 would substantially increase the grounds for inadmissibility on account of membership in a terrorist organization. Presently, membership in a *foreign terrorist organization designated by the Secretary of State under INA § 219*, or membership in an organization that the alien *knows or should have known* is a terrorist organization, makes an alien inadmissible.[72] H.R. 418 would facilitate the removal of a member of a non-designated terrorist organization by shifting the burden from the Government to show that the alien knew or should have known the nature of the organization to the alien to demonstrate *by clear and convincing evidence* that he did not know, and should not reasonably have known, that the organization was a terrorist organization.

Again, the proposed expansion of "terrorist organization" could significantly amplify the potential impact of these changes.

Officers, Spokesmen, and Representatives of the Palestine Liberation Organization

In both current law and H.R. 418, an alien who is an officer, official, representative, or spokesman of the Palestine Liberation Organization is inadmissible.

Expanding Inadmissibility Grounds for Espousal of Terrorist Activity

Under current law, aliens are inadmissible for the espousal of terrorist activity only if they (1) use positions of prominence (within any country) to endorse or espouse terrorist activity, or to persuade others to support terrorist activity or a terrorist organization, and (2) do so in a way that undermines U.S. efforts to reduce or eliminate terrorist activities, based on a determination by the Secretary of State. H.R. 418 would make inadmissible *any* alien who espouses or endorses terrorist activity, or persuades others to support terrorist activity or a terrorist organization, *regardless* of whether the alien has a position of prominence and his espousal undermines U.S. efforts to reduce terrorism in the opinion of the Secretary of State.

It is important to note that this ground for inadmissibility does not include a *mens rea* requirement. It appears that an alien who persuades others to support a terrorist organization would be deemed inadmissible even if the alien had no knowledge of the organization's terrorist activities. The possibility of this occurring may not be improbable, given H.R. 418's proposed expansion of the definition of "terrorist organization" to include any group that engages, or has a *subgroup* that engages in terrorist activity, including soliciting funds or otherwise providing material support for a "terrorist organization" (which itself may be one solely because it has, for example, a subgroup that has solicited or provided funds to another "terrorist organization").

Receiving Military-Type Training from or on Behalf of a Terrorist Organization

H.R. 418 would make inadmissible any alien who has received military-type training from or on behalf of any organization that, at the time the training was received, was a terrorist organization, a term defined under INA § 212(a)(3)(B)(vi) (and amended by H.R. 418 § 103(c)). Currently, the receipt of such training is only a deportable offense.[73] It is important to note that this ground for inadmissibility does not include a *mens rea* requirement, and does not specify that the organization must be designated as a terrorist organization by the United States.

Accordingly, it appears that an alien who receives military-type training from or on behalf of a terrorist organization would be inadmissible, regardless of whether the alien was aware or should have been aware that the organization was engaged in terrorist activity.

Inadmissibility of a Spouse or Child of an Alien Inadmissible on Terror-Related Grounds

H.R. 418 neither alters the inadmissibility of the spouse or child of an alien who was deemed inadmissible on terror-related grounds nor eliminates the current exception to inadmissibility for an alien's spouse or child who (1) did not and should not have reasonably known about the terrorist activity or (2) in the reasonable belief of the consular officer or Attorney General, has renounced the terror-related activity causing the alien to be found inadmissible.

Association with a Terrorist Organization

H.R. 418 does not amend INA § 212(a)(3)(F), which designates an alien as inadmissible if the Secretary of State, after consultation with the Attorney General, or the Attorney General, after consultation with the Secretary of State, determines that the alien has been associated with a terrorist organization and intends while in the United States to engage solely, principally, or incidentally in activities that could endanger the welfare, safety, or security of the United States.

Effective Date of Proposed Changes to the Terror-Related Grounds for Inadmissibility

Pursuant to § 103(c) of H.R. 418, the proposed changes to the terror-related grounds for inadmissibility would be effective on the date of H.R. 418's enactment, and apply to removal proceedings instituted before or after H.R. 418's enactment, as well as to acts and conditions constituting a ground for inadmissibility occurring or existing before or after H.R. 418's enactment.

Terror-Related Grounds for Deportability of Aliens

Aliens found to have engaged in terror-related activities following admission into the United States may be deportable. Presently, the terror-related grounds for inadmissibility are significantly broader than those for deportability.

Current Law

INA § 237(a)(4)(B) provides that an alien is deportable if he commits any of the actions falling under the INA's definition of "engage in terrorist activity." Pursuant to § 5402 of the Intelligence Reform and Terrorism Prevention Act of 2004, any alien who has received military-type training from or on behalf of any organization that, at the time the training was received, was designated as a terrorist organization by the Secretary of State, is deportable.[74]

Changes Proposed by H.R. 418

Section 104(a) of H.R. 418 would significantly expand the terror-related grounds for deportability, so that any alien who would be considered inadmissible under the provisions of INA §§ 212(a)(3)(B) (relating to terrorist activity) or 212(a)(3)(F) (relating to association with a terrorist organization) would also be deportable. The following sections discuss the new deportation grounds that would be added by H.R. 418, presuming that H.R. 418's provisions expanding the scope of INA § 212(a)(3)(B) (terror-related grounds for inadmissibility) were also enacted.

Effects of Expanded Definition of "Engage in Terrorist Activity" on Terror-Related Grounds for Deportability

A person who engages in terrorist activity is both inadmissible and deportable under current law. If H.R. 418 is enacted, this would remain the case. However, as previously mentioned, § 103(b) of H.R. 418 would also expand the applicable definition of the term "engage in terrorist activity." Thus, an alien who provided material support or solicited funds or participation in a non-designated terrorist organization would be deportable unless he demonstrated *by clear and convincing* evidence that he did not and should not have reasonably known that the organization was a terrorist organization.

Designation as Deportable for Terror-Related Activity by a Consular Officer, the Attorney General, or the Secretary of Homeland Security

H.R. 418 would enable a consular officer, the Attorney General, or the Secretary of Homeland Security to declare an alien inadmissible who is known to be engaged in terrorist activity or is likely to engage in such activity upon entry into the United States. Although H.R. 418 provides that "any alien considered inadmissible [on terror-related grounds]...is deportable,"[75] it is unclear whether this would mean that a consular officer, the Attorney General, or the Secretary of Homeland Security could declare an alien deportable if the alien was known to be engaged in terrorist activity or was likely to engage in such activity within the United States or what procedures would apply in such a circumstance.

Incitement of Terrorist Activity

H.R. 418 would make any alien who incited terrorist activity, under circumstances indicating an intention to cause death or serious bodily harm, deportable as well as inadmissible.

Representation of a Terrorist Organization or Political Group Espousing Terrorist Activity

H.R. 418 would make deportable as well as inadmissible any representative of either (1) a terrorist organization or (2) a political, social or other similar group that endorses or espouses terrorist activity.

Membership in a Terrorist Organization

H.R. 418 would make it a deportable offense for an alien to be either (1) a member of a terrorist organization designated by the Secretary of State, or (2) a member of any group that constitutes a terrorist organization, unless the alien can demonstrate *by clear and convincing* evidence, that he did not know, and should not reasonably have known, that the organization was a terrorist organization.

Officers, Spokesmen, and Representatives of the Palestine Liberation Organization

Pursuant to H.R. 418, an alien who is an officer, official, representative, or spokesman of the Palestine Liberation Organization would be made deportable.

Espousal of Terrorist Activity

An alien who espouses or endorses terrorist activity, or persuades others to support terrorist activity or a terrorist organization, would be deportable as well as inadmissible if H.R. 418 were enacted. As discussed previously, this ground for inadmissibility/deportability does not include a *mens rea* requirement, meaning that an alien who persuades others to support a terrorist organization would be considered deportable even if the alien had no knowledge of the organization's terrorist activities.

Receiving Military-Type Training from or on Behalf of a Terrorist Organization

Section 104(b) H.R. 418 would repeal the current grounds for deportability on account of receiving military-type training from or on behalf of a terrorist organization designated by the Secretary of State. Instead, the provision added by H.R. 418 making aliens who receive military-type training from or on behalf of *any* terrorist organization (i.e., not simply those designated as such by the Secretary of State) inadmissible would also be grounds for deporting an alien. Given H.R. 418's amendments to the INA's definition of "terrorist organization" and the terror-related grounds for inadmissibility, it appears that an alien who receives military-type training from or on behalf of a terrorist organization would be deportable regardless of whether the alien was aware that the organization was engaged in terrorist activity.

Deportability of a Spouse or Child of an Alien Inadmissible on Terror-Related Grounds

H.R. 418 would make the spouse or child of an alien inadmissible on terror-related grounds deportable, if the terror-related activity causing the alien to be inadmissible occurred within the last five years, unless the alien's spouse or child (1) did not and should not have reasonably known about the terrorist activity or (2) in the reasonable belief of the consular officer or Attorney General, has renounced the terror-related activity causing the alien to be found inadmissible.

Association with a Terrorist Organization as Grounds for Deportability

H.R. 418 would make an alien deportable on the same grounds that the alien would be inadmissible pursuant to INA § 212(a)(3)(F). Accordingly, an alien would be deportable if the Secretary of State, after consultation with the Attorney General, or the Attorney General, after consultation with the Secretary of State, determines that the alien has been associated with a terrorist organization and intends while in the United States to engage solely, principally, or incidentally in activities that could endanger the welfare, safety, or security of the United States.

Effective Date of Proposed Changes to the Terror-Related Grounds for Deportability

Pursuant to § 104(a)(2) of H.R. 418, the proposed changes to the terror-related grounds for deportability would be effective on the date of H.R. 418's enactment, and would apply to acts and conditions constituting a ground for removal occurring or existing before or after H.R. 418's enactment.

Consequences of Terror-Related Activities on Eligibility For Relief from Removal

An alien found to have engaged in terror-related activities is not only inadmissible and potentially deportable, but is also ineligible for various forms of relief from removal. In modifying the terror-related grounds for inadmissibility and deportability, H.R. 418 would also affect certain aliens' eligibility for relief from removal. Specifically, H.R. 418 would expand the scope of aliens who were ineligible for asylum, withholding of removal, and cancellation of removal.

Asylum

Asylum is a discretionary form of relief from removal available to aliens in the U.S. who have a well-founded fear of persecution on account of race, religion, nationality, membership in a particular social group, or political opinion. Aliens who have been admitted into the U.S. or who entered surreptitiously are generally in the posture of potentially "deportable" aliens and removable under grounds for deportation. Aliens otherwise present in the U.S. — "paroled" aliens and aliens presently arriving at an airport or other port of entry, for example — are in the posture of potentially "inadmissible" aliens and removable under the grounds for inadmissibility.

Aliens engaged in terrorist activity are ineligible for asylum, as are aliens who fall under most other terrorism provisions. Mere membership in a terrorist organization is perhaps the most notable exception to this automatic disqualification. H.R. 418 would preserve this exception for inadmissible aliens, but as explained below, it might, as presently drafted, deny this exemption to deportable aliens. Other changes in current law also might result due to changes in cross-references and section numbering arising from H.R. 418.

Current Restrictions on Asylum Eligibility for Aliens Deportable on Terror-Related Grounds

Presently, a *deportable* alien is ineligible for asylum relief on terror-related grounds if he is "removable under [INA] § 237(a)(4)(B) (relating to terrorist activity)." Presently, an alien is removable under § 237(a)(4)(B) only if he commits certain actions defined as "engaging in terrorist activity" under INA § 212(a)(3)(B)(iv). As previously mentioned, "engaging in terrorist activity" is only one of several terror-related grounds under which an alien may be deemed *inadmissible.*

H.R. 418's Effects upon Asylum Eligibility Restrictions for Aliens Deportable on Terror-Related Grounds

INA § 208(b)(2)(A)(v) currently makes ineligible for asylum any alien who is (1) *inadmissible* on specified terrorism grounds (those terror-related grounds for inadmissibility provided under subclause (I), (II), (III), (IV), and (VI) of INA § 212 (a)(3)(B)(i)) or (2) *deportable* under INA § 237(a)(4)(B) (relating to terrorist activity). With regard to (2), H.R. 418 would amend INA § 237(a)(4)(B), so that a deportable alien would not only be deportable for engaging in terrorist activity, but also for committing terror-related activity that would make the alien inadmissible under INA § 212 — including those activities that do not make an alien who is *inadmissible* on terror-related grounds ineligible for asylum. Accordingly, if enacted in its present form, H.R. 418 would appear to create a disparity in asylum eligibility, under which an alien designated as *inadmissible* on account of certain terror-related activities, would be eligible for asylum relief, while an alien who was *deportable* on the same grounds would be ineligible.

Pursuant to amendments made by H.R. 418, which do not directly alter the INA's asylum eligibility provisions but do make the terror-related grounds for deportability the same as those for inadmissibility, a *deportable* alien would be ineligible for asylum on terror-related grounds if:

the alien has engaged in a terrorist activity;

a consular officer, the Attorney General, or the Secretary of Homeland Security knows, or has reasonable ground to believe, that the alien is engaged in or is likely to engage after entry in any terrorist activity;

the alien has, under circumstances indicating an intention to cause death or serious bodily harm, incited terrorist activity;

the alien is a representative of a terrorist organization, or a political, social or other similar group that endorses or espouses terrorist activity;

the alien is a member of a group designated as a terrorist organization by the United States;

the alien is a member of a group of two or more individuals, whether organized or not, that engages in, or has a subgroup that engages in a terrorist activity, *unless* the alien can demonstrate *by clear and convincing* evidence that the alien did not know, and should not reasonably have known, that the organization was a terrorist organization;

the alien endorses or espouses terrorist activity or persuades others to endorse or espouse terrorist activity or support a terrorist organization (possibly including an organization that the alien does not know has engaged in terrorist activities, but nevertheless meets the INA's definition of "terrorist organization");

the alien has received military-type training from or on behalf of any organization that, at the time the training was received, was a terrorist organization (possibly including an organization that the alien does not know to engage in terrorist activities, but nevertheless meets the INA's definition of "terrorist organization");

a spouse or child of an alien who is inadmissible on terror-related grounds, if the activity causing the alien to be found inadmissible occurred within the last five years, *unless* the spouse or child (1) did not and should not have reasonably known about the terrorist activity or (2) in the reasonable belief of the consular officer or Attorney General, has renounced the terror-related activity causing the alien to be found inadmissible; or

the Secretary of State, after consultation with the Attorney General, or the Attorney General, after consultation with the Secretary of State, determines that the alien has been associated with a terrorist organization and intends while in the United States to engage solely, principally, or incidentally in activities that could endanger the welfare, safety, or security of the United States.[76]

Current Restrictions on Asylum Eligibility for Aliens Inadmissible on Terror-Related Grounds

Pursuant to INA § 208(b)(2)(A)(v), an *inadmissible* alien is ineligible for asylum only if the alien "is inadmissible under subclause (I), (II), (III), (IV), or (VI) of [INA] § 212(a)(3)(B)(i)." Under current law, an inadmissible alien would be denied eligibility on terror-related grounds if:

he has engaged in a terrorist activity (subclause I);

a consular officer or the Attorney General knows, or has reasonable ground to believe, that the alien is engaged in or is likely to engage after entry in any terrorist activity (subclause II);

the alien has incited terrorist activity, under circumstances indicating an intention to cause death or serious bodily harm (subclause III);

the alien is a representative of a foreign terrorist organization designated by the Secretary of State under INA § 219 or a political, social or other similar group whose public endorsement of acts of terrorist activity the Secretary of State has determined undermines United States efforts to reduce or eliminate terrorist activities, *unless* the Attorney General determines, in the Attorney General's discretion, that there are not reasonable grounds for regarding the alien as a danger to the security of the United States (subclause IV);[77] or

the alien has used the alien's position of prominence within any country to endorse or espouse terrorist activity, or to persuade others to support terrorist activity or a terrorist organization, in a way that the Secretary of State has determined undermines United States efforts to reduce or eliminate terrorist activities (subclause VI).[78]

Changes to Asylum Eligibility for Inadmissible Aliens Made by H.R. 418

INA § 208(b)(2)(A)(v) makes ineligible for asylum any alien who "is inadmissible under subclause (I), (II), (III), (IV), or (VI) of [INA] § 212(a)(3)(B)(i)" (terror-related grounds for alien inadmissibility). As discussed previously, § 103(a) of H.R. 418 would significantly modify INA § 212(a)(3)(B)(i) by *amending and rearranging* the terror-related grounds for inadmissibility found in INA § 212(a)(3)(B)(i). For example, whereas under current law subclause (VI) of INA § 212(a)(3)(B)(i) makes inadmissible (and also ineligible for asylum, when as referenced by INA § 208(b)(2)(A)(v)) any alien who has used his position of prominence to endorse or espouse terrorist activity, pursuant to the amendments made by H.R. 418, subclause (VI) would instead describe the inadmissibility ground for aliens who are members of non-designated terrorist organizations (espousal of terrorist activity would still be a ground for inadmissibility, but would now be found in subclause

(VII) of INA § 212(a)(3)(B)(i)). By rearranging and amending the INA provisions relating to the terror-related grounds for inadmissibility, H.R. 418 would affect the scope of the terror-related grounds for asylum ineligibility that refer to those amended provisions.

If H.R. 418 is enacted in its current form, asylum eligibility would continue to be denied only those aliens who are *inadmissible* under subclause (I), (II), (III), (IV), or (VI) of INA § 212(a)(3)(B). Pursuant to the amendments proposed by H.R. 418 to the terror-related grounds for inadmissibility, which amend and rearrange the terror-related grounds for inadmissibility described in INA § 212(a)(3)(B), an *inadmissible* alien would be denied asylum on terror-related grounds if:

the alien has engaged in a terrorist activity (subclause I, as amended);

a consular officer, the Attorney General, or the Secretary of Homeland Security knows, or has reasonable ground to believe, that the alien is engaged in or is likely to engage after entry in any terrorist activity (subclause II, as amended);

the alien has, under circumstances indicating an intention to cause death or serious bodily harm, incited terrorist activity (subclause III, as amended);

the alien is a representative of a terrorist organization, or a political, social or other similar group that endorses or espouses terrorist activity, unless the Attorney General determines, in the Attorney General's discretion, that there are not reasonable grounds for regarding the alien as a danger to the security of the United States (subclause IV, as amended); or

the alien is a member of non-designated terrorist organization, whether organized or not, which engages in, or has a subgroup which engages in a terrorist activity, *unless* the alien can demonstrate *by clear and convincing* evidence that the alien did not know, and should not reasonably have known, that the organization was a terrorist organization (subclause VI, as amended).[79]

Because of the manner in which H.R. 418 would amend the INA provision concerning the terror-related grounds for inadmissibility, an inadmissible alien would no longer be automatically ineligible for asylum if he has used a position of prominence to endorse or espouse terrorist activity (although, as discussed previously, a *deportable* alien would be ineligible for asylum on such grounds).[80] On the other hand, membership in a non-designated terrorist organization would automatically deny an alien eligibility for asylum relief, unless the alien could demonstrate *by clear and convincing* evidence that the alien did not know, and should not reasonably have known, that the organization was a terrorist organization.

Withholding of Removal

Apart from asylum is the separate remedy of withholding of removal. Like asylum, withholding of removal is premised upon a showing of prospective persecution of an alien if removed to a particular country.[81] In certain circumstances, aliens are ineligible for withholding of removal, including in cases where the Attorney General decides:

that having been convicted by a final judgment of a particularly serious crime, an alien is a danger to the community of the United States;

there are serious reasons to believe that the alien committed a serious nonpolitical crime outside the United States before the alien arrived in the United States; or

that there are reasonable grounds to believe that the alien is a danger to the security of the United States.[82]

By statute, an alien who is described in INA § 237(a)(4)(B) (i.e., is engaged or has engaged in terrorist activity) is reasonably regarded as a danger to the security of the United States, and is therefore ineligible for withholding of removal.[83]

Current Restrictions on Withholding of Removal Eligibility for Aliens Deportable on Terror-Related Grounds

Presently, an alien lawfully admitted into the United States is ineligible for withholding of removal on terror-related grounds only if he is deportable under INA § 237(a)(4)(B), which makes an alien deportable if he is "engaged in terrorist activity," as defined under INA § 212(a)(3)(B)(iv).

H.R. 418's Effects upon Withholding of Removal Eligibility for Aliens Deportable on Terror-Related Grounds

H.R. 418 would amend INA § 237(a)(4)(B) to make an alien deportable on the same terror-related grounds that make an alien inadmissible. Because H.R. 418 does not modify the present wording of the INA's withholding of removal eligibility requirements, an alien who is removable pursuant to any of the expanded, terror-related grounds for deportability would also be ineligible for withholding of removal.

Current Restrictions on Withholding of Removal Eligibility for Aliens Inadmissible on Terror-Related Grounds

The INA does not specify that aliens who are inadmissible on terror-related grounds are automatically ineligible for withholding of removal, though they might nevertheless fulfill the criteria for relief ineligibility. Currently, for example, an alien who is *deportable* on the grounds that he has engaged in terrorist activity is ineligible for withholding of removal on account of the danger he likely poses to the United States.[84] An alien who is *inadmissible* on account of engaging in terrorist activity would be ineligible for withholding of removal for the same reason.

H.R. 418's Effects upon Withholding of Removal Eligibility for Aliens Inadmissible on Terror-Related Grounds

H.R. 418 would appear to make aliens who are inadmissible on terror-related grounds ineligible for withholding of removal. INA § 241(b)(3) provides that an alien who is *described* by INA § 237(a)(3)(B) is ineligible for withholding of removal. H.R. 418 amends § 237(a)(3)(B) to cover any alien who would be considered inadmissible on terror related grounds.[85] Accordingly, it would appear that if H.R. 418 was enacted, an alien who is inadmissible on terror-related grounds would also be ineligible for withholding of removal.

Cancellation of Removal

The INA provides the Attorney General with the discretionary authority to cancel the removal of certain permanent and nonpermanent residents. However, aliens who are inadmissible or deportable on account of terrorrelated activity are ineligible for such relief.

Current Restrictions on Cancellation of Removal Eligibility for Aliens Deportable on Terror-Related Grounds

An alien is ineligible for cancellation of removal if he is deportable under INA § 237(a)(4).[86] Presently, the only terror-related grounds under which an alien would be expressly ineligible for cancellation of removal would be if the alien either engaged in terrorist activity, as defined by INA § 212(a)(3)(B)(iv) or received military-type training from or on behalf of a designated terrorist organization.[87]

H.R. 418's Effects upon Cancellation of Removal Eligibility for Aliens Deportable on Terror-Related Grounds

H.R. 418 would amend INA § 237(a)(4)(B) so that any alien who would be considered inadmissible on terror-related grounds (as amended by H.R. 418) would also be deportable, significantly increasing the terror-related grounds that may disqualify a deportable alien from having his removal canceled.

Current Restrictions on Cancellation of Removal Eligibility for Aliens Inadmissible on Terror-Related Grounds

An alien is ineligible for cancellation of removal if he is inadmissible under INA § 212(a)(3), which contains both security and terror-related grounds for inadmissibility.

H.R. 418's Effects upon Cancellation of Removal Eligibility for Aliens Inadmissible on Terror-Related Grounds

As discussed previously, H.R. 418 would amend INA § 212(a)(3)(B)(i) to broaden the terror-related grounds for inadmissibility. Accordingly, the category of inadmissible aliens who would be ineligible for cancellation of removal on terror-related grounds would be expanded.

IV. IMPROVED SECURITY FOR DRIVERS' LICENSES AND PERSONAL IDENTIFICATION CARDS [88]

Prior to the passage of the Intelligence Reform and Terrorism Prevention Act of 2004, standards with respect to drivers' licenses and personal identification cards were determined on a state-by-state basis with no national standards in place.[89] Even with the passage of the Intelligence Reform and Terrorism Prevention Act of 2004, it appears that, with the exception of what is specifically provided for by the legislation, a majority of the standards remain at the discretion of state and local governments.[90]

H.R. 418 contains a number of provisions relating to improved security for drivers' licenses and personal identification cards, as well as instructions for states that do not comply with its provisions. H.R. 418 would also repeal certain overlapping and potentially conflicting provisions of the Intelligence Reform and Terrorism Prevention Act of 2004.[91]

Current Law

The Intelligence Reform and Terrorism Prevention Act of 2004 delegates authority to the Secretary of Transportation, in consultation with the Secretary of Homeland Security, empowering them to issue regulations with respect to minimum standards for federal acceptance of drivers' licenses and personal identification cards.[92]

The new law requires that the Secretary issue regulations within 18 months of enactment that require each driver's license or identification card, to be accepted for any official purpose by a federal agency, to include the individual's: (1) full legal name; (2) date of birth; (3) gender; (4) driver's license or identification card number; (5) digital photograph; (6) address; and (7) signature.[93] In addition, the cards are required to contain physical security features designed to prevent tampering, counterfeiting or duplication for fraudulent purposes; as well as a common machine readable technology with defined minimum elements.[94] Moreover, states will be required, pursuant to the new regulations, to confiscate a driver's license or personal identification card if any of the above security components is compromised.[95]

The statute also requires that the regulations address how drivers' licences and identification cards are issued by the states. Specifically, the regulations are required to include minimum standards for the documentation required by the applicant, the procedures utilized for verifying the documents used, and the standards for processing the applications.[96] The regulations are, however, prohibited from not only infringing upon the "State's power to set criteria concerning what categories of individuals are eligible to obtain a driver's license or personal identification card from that State,"[97] but also from requiring a state to take an action that "conflicts with or otherwise interferes with the full enforcement of state criteria concerning the categories of individuals that are eligible to obtain a driver's license or personal identification card."[98] In other words, it would appear that if a state grants a certain category of individuals (i.e., aliens, legal or illegal) permission to obtain a license, nothing in the forthcoming regulations is to infringe on that state's decision or its ability to enforce that decision. In addition, the regulations are also not to require a single uniform design, and must include procedures designed to protect the privacy rights of individual applicants.[99]

Finally, the law requires the use of negotiated rulemaking pursuant to the Administrative Procedure Act.[100] This process is designed to bring together agency representatives and concerned interest groups to negotiate the text of a proposed rule. The rulemaking committee is required to include representatives from: (1) state and local offices that issue drivers' licenses and/or personal identification cards; (2) state elected officials; (3) Department of Homeland Security; and (4) interested parties.[101]

Changes Proposed by H.R. 418

In general, the provisions of H.R. 418 appear to effectively (though not explicitly) preempt state and local laws and regulations regarding drivers' licenses and personal identification cards in favor of specific national standards established by statute and forthcoming corresponding regulations.[102] In addition, H.R. 418 contains a provision that specifically repeals the recently enacted § 7212 of the Intelligence Reform and Terrorism Prevention Act of 2004, which contains the current law with respect to national standards for drivers' licenses and personal identification cards.

Minimum Issuance Standards

Section 202(c) of H.R. 418 would establish minimum issuance standards for federal recognition requiring that before a state could issue a driver's license or photo identification card, a state would have to verify with the issuing agency, the issuance, validity and completeness of: (1) a photo identification document or a non-photo document containing both the individual's full legal name and date of birth; (2) date of birth; (3) proof of a social security number (SSN) or verification of the individual's ineligibility for a SSN; and (4) name and address of the individual's principal residence. To the extent that information verification requirements exist, they are currently a function of state law and likely vary from state to state. This provision would appear to preempt any state verification standards and replace them with the new federal standards as established by this statutory language.

Evidence of Legal Status

Section 202(c)(2)(B) of H.R. 418 appears to require states to verify an applicant's legal status in the United States before issuing a driver's license or personal identification card. Currently, the categories of persons eligible for drivers' licenses are determined on a state-by-state basis. As indicated above, the Intelligence Reform and Terrorist Prevention Act of 2004 specifically prevents the Secretary of Transportation from enacting regulations that would interfere with this authority. If enacted, this section of H.R. 418 would appear to preempt any state law requirements and appears to require the states to verify the legal status of the applicant.[103]

Temporary Drivers' Licenses and Identification Cards

Section 202(c)(2)(C) of H.R. 418 establishes a system of temporary licenses and identification cards that can be issued by the states to applicants who can present evidence that they fall into one of six categories.[104] Under H.R. 418, a state may only issue a temporary driver's license or identification card with an expiration date equal to the period of time of the applicant's authorized stay in the United States. If there is an indefinite end to the period of authorized stay, the card's expiration date shall be one year. The temporary card shall clearly indicate that it is temporary and shall state the expiration date. Renewals of the temporary cards would be done only upon presentation of valid documentary evidence that the status had been extended by the Secretary of Homeland Security. If such provisions exist under current law, they exist as a function of state law and would be preempted should H.R. 418 get enacted.

Applications for Renewal, Duplication, or Re-Issuance

Section 202(c)(3) of H.R. 418 requires, in instances of renewal, duplication, or re-issuance of a driver's license or identification card, that a state presume that the initial card was issued in accordance with the law, if at the time of application, the driver's license or identification card has not expired or been canceled, suspended or revoked. This presumption would be inapplicable if the state is notified by a local, state or federal government agency that the individual seeking renewal, duplication or re-issuance is neither a citizen of the United States nor legally present in the United States. Like issuance standards, currently renewal, duplication and re-issuance standards are governed by state law and may vary on a state-by-state basis. Should H.R. 418 be enacted into law, it would appear that these state provisions would be preempted in favor of the new federally developed standards.

Other Requirements

Pursuant to § 202(d) of H.R. 418, states are required to adopt procedures and practices to: (1) employ technology to capture digital images of identity source documents; (2) retain paper copies of source documents for a minimum of seven years or images of source documents presented for a minimum of ten years; (3) subject each applicant to a mandatory facial image capture; (4) confirm or verify a renewing applicant's information; (5) confirm with the

Social Security Administration a SSN presented by a person using the full Social Security account number;[105] (6) refuse issuance of a driver's license or identification card to a person holding a driver's license issued by another state without confirmation that the person is terminating or has terminated the driver's license; (7) ensure the physical security of locations where cards are produced and the security of document materials and papers from which drivers' licenses and identification cards are produced; (8) subject all persons authorized to manufacture or produce drivers' licenses and identification cards to appropriate security clearance requirements; (9) establish fraudulent document recognition training programs for appropriate employees engaged in the issuance of drivers' licenses and identification cards; (10) would limit the length of time a drivers' license or personal identification card is valid to eight years. To the extent that any of these requirements currently exist, they do so as a function of state law. Thus, should H.R. 418 be enacted, it would appear that the state laws would be preempted in favor of the new federal standards.

Alternative Issuance Provision

H.R. 418 also addresses the potential situation where a state issues a driver's license or personal identification card that does not comply with H.R. 418's provisions. Should that situation arise, section 202(d)(11) requires not only that the card clearly indicate that the card is not to be accepted for official purposes by federal agencies, but also that any card not in compliance use a "unique design or color indicator" as a means of alerting federal agents that the card is unacceptable for official purposes. While this provision appears to preserve a state's ability to continue to issue drivers' licenses and identification cards that do not comply with the federal standards, it nevertheless also appears to place an affirmative obligation on the state to notify federal agents of the decision to issue non-compliant licenses and identification cards.[106]

Additional Powers of the Secretary

Section 202(d) of H.R. 418 appears to provide discretionary authority to the Secretary of Homeland Security, authorizing the prescription of "one or more design formats for driver's licenses and identification cards" to protect national security and to allow for visual differentiation between categories or licenses and identification cards. In addition, H.R. 418 provides the Secretary of Homeland Security with discretionary authority to further limit the length of validity of licenses and identifications cards for the purpose of periodically confirming address and evidence of lawful residence in the United States.

Current law leaves both the design formats and the length of validity determination to the discretion of the individual sovereign states. H.R. 418, if enacted, would appear to preempt these state laws and regulations in favor of a uniform federal standards.

Linking of Databases

Section 203 of H.R. 418 provides that for a state to be eligible for any grant funding or other available federal assistance under this title it must participate in the Interstate Drivers' License Compact and provide electronic access to its motor vehicle databases to all other participants. In addition, H.R. 418 requires that all motor vehicle databases are to contain, at a minimum, all of the data printed on a state driver's license and all motor vehicle histories including moving violations, suspensions and points on licenses. Currently, the Interstate Drivers License Compact requires member states to report tickets received by a motorist to the state where he received a license to drive so that the driver receives the required points on his license. Also, when a state suspends the license of a driver who is from out-of-state, the state where the motorist received a license to drive will also suspend the license. The compact operates as a function of state law and has been approved by Congress pursuant to the Interstate Compacts Clause.[107] It appears that 46 states and the District of Columbia are currently members of the compact and therefore would remain eligible for federal grant money.[108]

Trafficking in Authentication Features for Use in False Identification Documents

Section 204 of H.R. 418 amends 18 U.S.C. § 1028(a)(8), which makes it a federal crime to either actually, or with the intent to, transport, transfer, or otherwise dispose of to another, materials or features[109] used on a document of the type intended or commonly used for identification purposes. By replacing the phrase "false identification features" with "false or actual authentication features," this provision would appear to broaden the scope of the criminal provision, making it a crime to traffic in identification features regardless of whether the feature is false.

References

[1] See generally CRS Report RL32169, Immigration Legislation and Issues in the 108th Congress, Andorra Bruno, Coordinator.

[2] Pub. L. No. 108-458, 118 Stat. 3638 (2004). For further background, see CRS Report RL32616, 9/11 Commission: Legislative Action Concerning U.S. Immigration Law and Policy in the 108th Congress, by Michael John Garcia and Ruth Ellen Wasem.

[3] See Mary Curtius, The Nation; GOP Congressman Renews Push for Immigration Curbs, L.A. TIMES, Jan. 27, 2005, at A18.

[4] Reportedly, H.R. 368 was introduced by Rep. Davis so that the House could consider the identification document provisions contained in H.R. 418 separately. Patrick O'Connor, Sensenbrenner and Davis Bills Square Off, THE HILL, Feb. 1, 2005, at 1, 6.

[5] Discussion of this topic was prepared by Margaret Mikyung Lee, Legislative Attorney.

[6] FINAL REPORT OF THE NATIONAL COMMISSION ON TERRORIST ATTACKS UPON THE UNITED STATES, July 2004.

[7] E.g. at 72. Ramzi Yousef, one of the terrorists involved in the 1993 World Trade Center bombing, entered the United States on a political asylum claim.

[8] Pub. L. No. 104-132, 110 Stat. 1214 (1996).

[9] Division C of Pub. L. No. 104-208, 110 Stat. 3009-546 (1996).

[10] 8 U.S.C. §§ 1101 et seq.

[11] 8 U.S.C. § 1158(b).

[12] 8 U.S.C. § 1101(A)(42)(A).

[13] See INA § 203(a)(7) between Pub. L. No. 89-236, 79 Stat. 911 (1965) and Pub .L. No. 96-212, 94 Stat. 109 (1980), [current version at 8 U.S.C. § 1153(a)(7)] and Shubash v. District Director, 450 F.2d 345 (9th Cir. 1971).

[14] C. Gordon, S. Mailman, & S. Yale-Loehrer, IMMIGRATION LAW & PROCEDURE, § 34.02 (2004) (hereinafter IMMIGRATION LAW & PROCEDURE).

[15] See id. § 34.02[9] for a discussion of the case law concerning evidentiary standards.

[16] "It is well established in this circuit that the BIA may not require independent corroborative evidence from an asylum applicant who testifies credibly in support of his application. . . . It is also well settled that we must accept an applicant's testimony as true in the absence of an explicit adverse credibility finding." Kataria v. INS, 232 F.3d 1107, 1113-14 (9th Cir. 2000) (citations omitted). "Even under the substantial evidence standard, an adverse credibility finding must be based on 'specific cogent reasons,' which are substantial and 'bear a legitimate

nexus to the finding.'" Cordon-Garcia v. INS, 204 F.3d 985, 993 (9th Cir. 2000).

[17] Sidhu v. INS, 220 F.3d 1085, 1092 (9th Cir. 2000).

[18] In re S-M-J-, Applicant, 21 I. & N. Dec. 722, 1997 WL 80984 (B.I.A. 1997).

[19] Ladha v. I.N.S., 215 F.3d 889 (9th Cir. 2000).

[20] See IMMIGRATION LAW & PROCEDURE § 34.02[9][c][ii][B], notes 288-292 and accompanying text.

[21] "[I]nternational standards do not conflict with the BIA's expectation of corroborating evidence in certain cases. The Handbook of the United Nations High Commissioner for Refugees notes that applicants should 'make an effort to support [their] statements by any available evidence and give a satisfactory explanation for any lack of evidence.'" Diallo v. INS, 232 F.3d 279, 286 (2nd Cir. 2000).

[22] While such a person may have applied for asylum, CRS has not found an instance in which such a person was granted asylum.

[23] 8 U.S.C. § 1158(b)(1).

[24] Pub. L. No. 107-296, §§ 1102, 1502, 116 Stat. 2135, 2273, 2308, as amended by Pub. L. No. 108-7, Div. L, § 105(a), 117 Stat. 11, 531 (2003).

[25] At [http://www.whitehouse.gov/news/releases/2002/11/reorganization_plan.pdf], last visited Jan. 13, 2005.

[26] IMMIGRATION LAW AND PROCEDURE § 33.04 (2004), comparing, e.g., Fadul v. INS, No. 99-2029, 2000 U.S. App. LEXIS 4952 (7th Cir. Mar. 20, 2000) (death threats by the New People's Army motivated by extortion efforts, not political opinion) with Chen v. Ashcroft, 289 F.3d 1113, 1116 (9th Cir. 2002) (vacated on grounds unrelated to the motive analysis, 314 F.3d 995 (9th Cir. 2002)) ("It is not necessary that persecution be solely on account of one of the forbidden grounds for an asylum applicant to secure asylum. It is enough that a principal reason for the persecution be on account of a statutory ground"). See also Singh v. Ashcroft, 2004 U.S. App. LEXIS 18925, at *5 (9th Cir., Sept. 3, 2004); Agbuya v. INS, 241 F.3d 1224, 1228 (9th Cir. 2001); Borja v. INS, 175 F.3d 732, 734-36 (9th Cir. 1999) (en banc) (" . . . 'the plain meaning of the phrase 'persecution on account of the victim's political opinion,' does not mean persecution solely on account of the victim's political opinion. That is, the conclusion that a cause of persecution is economic does not necessarily imply that there cannot exist other causes of the persecution.' As the

United Nations' Handbook on Procedures and Criteria for Determining Refugee Status says, 'What appears at first sight to be primarily an economic motive for departure may in reality also involve a political element, and it may be the political opinions of the individual that expose him to serious consequences, rather than his objections to the economic measures themselves.' (quoting U.N. Handbook at §§ 62-64). To quote the Board's decision in this case, 'An applicant for asylum need not show conclusively why persecution occurred in the past or is likely to occur in the future. However, the applicant must produce evidence from which it is reasonable to believe that the harm was motivated, at least in part, by an actual or implied protected ground.'" (other cites omitted, emphasis added)); Singh v. Ilchert, 63 F.3d 1501, 1509 (9th Cir. 1995) ("Persecutory conduct may have more than one motive, and so long as one motive is one of the statutory grounds, the requirements have been satisfied."). See also CRS Report RL32621, U.S. Immigration Policy on Asylum Seekers, by Ruth Ellen Wasem, at 8, 22.

[27] 8 U.S.C. § 1231(b)(3).

[28] Compare INS v. Cardoza-Fonseca, 480 U.S. 421 (1987) with INS v. Stevic, 467 U.S. 407 (1984).

[29] 8 U.S.C. § 1159(b).

[30] 8 U.S.C. § 1158(b)(3).

[31] See IMMIGRATION LAW & PROCEDURE § 34.02[11][c].

[32] The Ninth Circuit has held that with regard to withholding of deportation/removal, administrative adjudicators improperly denied the application for lack of corroboration where the applicant gave credible testimony. E.g., Mendoza Manimboa v. Ashcroft, 329 F.3d 655 (9th Cir. 2003); Cajura-Flores v. Immigration and Naturalization Service, 784 F.2d 885 (9th Cir. 1985).

[33] 8 U.S.C. § 1227(a)(4)(B).

[34] 8 U.S.C. § 1231(b)(3).

[35] Again, the burden of proof is "clear probability of persecution" in withholding cases.

[36] 8 U.S.C. § 1252(b)(4).

[37] IMMIGRATION LAW & PROCEDURE § 34.02[12][g].

[38] Id. § 33.06[8].

[39] 8 U.S.C. § 1252(b)(4).

[40] E.g., Hoxha v. Ashcroft, 319 F.3d 1179 (9th Cir. 2003).

[41] 8 U.S.C. § 1252(a)(2).

[42] 8 U.S.C. § 1252(a)(2)(B).

[43] 8 U.S.C. § 1252(a)(2)(B)(ii).

[44] Discussion of this topic was prepared by Margaret Mikyung Lee, Legislative Attorney.

[45] 16 U.S.C. §§ 1531 et seq.

[46] 42 U.S.C. §§ 4321 et seq.

[47] See CRS Report RS22026, Border Security: Fences Along the U.S. International Border, by Blas Nuñez-Neto and Stephen R. Viña.

[48] 16 U.S.C. §§ 1451-1464.

[49] See California Coastal Commission, W8a Staff Report and Recommendation on Consistency Determination, CD-063-03, October 2003, at 14.

[50] This provision appears to address concerns raised during debate in the House of Representatives that providing for a waiver of all laws would result in a spate of lawsuits challenging the provision that would further delay construction. 151 Cong. Rec. H8899 (daily edition Oct. 8, 2004) (statement of Rep. Farr).

[51] Discussion of this topic was prepared by Michael John Garcia, Legislative Attorney.

[52] For further background, see CRS Report RL32564, Immigration: Terrorist Grounds for Exclusion of Aliens, by Michael John Garcia.

[53] INA § 212(a)(3)(B)(iii); 8 U.S.C. § 1182(a)(3)(B)(iii) (defining "terrorist activity").

[54] INA §§ 212(a)(3)(B)(i)(I), 237(a)(4)(B); 8 U.S.C. §§ 1182(a)(3)(B)(i)(I), 1227(a)(4)(B).

[55] INA § 212(a)(3)(B)(iv); 8 U.S.C. § 1182(a)(3)(B)(iv).

[56] INA § 212(a)(3)(B)(iv)(IV)-(VI); 8 U.S.C. § 1182(a)(3)(B)(iv)(IV)-(VI). If an alien provides material support for, or solicits funding or participation in, a terrorist activity or a group designated as a terrorist organization by the United States, he is deemed to have engaged in terrorist activity.

[57] INA § 212(a)(3)(B)(iv)(VI); 8 U.S.C. § 1182(a)(3)(B)(iv)(VI).

[58] INA § 212(a)(3)(B)(iv)(IV)-(VI); 8 U.S.C. § 1182(a)(3)(B)(iv)(IV)-(VI).

[59] Under H.R. 418, if an alien solicits funding or participation or material support for either a terrorist activity or a group designated as a terrorist organization by the United States, he is deemed to have engaged in terrorist activity. See H.R. 418 § 103(b). This standard is the same as that found in current law.

[60] The USA PATRIOT Act amended INA § 212 to expand the definition of "terrorist organization" to potentially include terrorist organizations not designated by the Secretary of State pursuant to INA § 219.

[61] See INA §§ 212(a)(3)(B)(i)(IV)-(V), 212(a)(3)(F); 8 U.S.C. §§ 1182 (a)(3)(B)(i)(IV)-(V), 1182(a)(3)(F).

[62] For further discussion of this provision, see CRS Report RL32120; The 'FTO List' and Congress: Sanctioning Designated Foreign Terrorist Organizations, by Audrey Kurth Cronin.

[63] INA § 212(a)(3)(B)(vi); 8 U.S.C. § 1182 (a)(3)(B)(vi).

[64] See INA § 212(a)(3)(B)(vi)(III); 8 U.S.C. § 1182 (a)(3)(B)(vi)(III).

[65] INA § 212(a); 8 U.S.C. § 1182(a).

[66] 8 U.S.C. § 1182(a)(3)(B)(i).

[67] The limited exception to inadmissibility for the spouse and child of an alien who is inadmissible on terror-related grounds is found in INA § 212(a)(3)(B)(ii).

[68] H.R. 418, § 103(a).

[69] INA § 212(a)(3)(B)(i)(II); 8 U.S.C. § 1182(a)(3)(B)(i)(II).

[70] H.R. 418, § 103(a).

[71] INA § 212(a)(3)(B)(i)(IV); 8 U.S.C. § 1182(a)(3)(B)(i)(IV).

[72] INA § 212(a)(3)(B)(i)(V); 8 U.S.C. § 1182(a)(3)(B)(i)(V).

[73] See INA § 237(a)(4)(E); 8 U.S.C. § 1227(a)(4)(E) (as amended by the Intelligence Reform and Terrorist Prevention Act of 2004, Pub. L. No. 108-458, § 5402).

[74] Id.

[75] H.R. 418, § 104(a).

[76] Id. §§ 103(a) (proposing amendments to the terror-related grounds for inadmissibility found in INA § 212(a)(B)(i)), 104(a); INA § 212(a)(3)(F), 8 U.S.C. § 1182(a)(3)(F).

[77] This exception exists because of the express language of INA § 208(b)(2)(v), which provides that an alien is ineligible for asylum if "the alien is inadmissible under subclause (I), (II), (III), (IV), or (VI) of [INA] § 212(a)(3)(B)(i)...unless, in the case only of an alien inadmissible under subclause (IV)...the Attorney General determines, in the Attorney General's discretion, that there are not reasonable grounds for regarding the alien as a danger to the security of the United States."

[78] INA § 208(b)(2)(A)(v); 8 U.S.C. § 1158(b)(2)(A)(v).

[79] See H.R. 418 § 103(amending the terror-related grounds for inadmissibility and the INA's definition of "terrorist organization" and "engage in terrorist activity").

[80] Compare INA § 212(a)(3)(B)(i)(VI) with H.R. 418 § 103(a) (amending and rearranging the terror-related grounds for inadmissibility).

[81] See INA § 241(b)(3); 8 U.S.C. § 1231(b)(3). See also 8 C.F.R. § 208.16.

[82] INA § 241(b)(3)(B); 8 U.S.C. § 1231(b)(3)(B).

[83] Id.

[84] Id.

[85] H.R. 418, § 104(a)(1).

[86] INA § 240A(c)(4); 8 U.S.C. § 1229b(c)(4).

[87] See INA § 237(a)(4); 8 U.S.C. § 1227(a)(4). A deportable alien involved in terror-related activity might nevertheless be ineligible for cancellation of removal on security or foreign policy grounds. See INA §§ 237(a)(4)(A), (C); 8 U.S.C. §§ 1227(a)(4)(A), (C).

[88] Discussion of this topic was prepared by Todd B. Tatelman, Legislative Attorney.

[89] Congressional action prior to 9/11 on national standards in this direction proved highly controversial. For example, § 656 of the Illegal Immigration Reform and Immigrant Responsibility Act of 1996 (Pub. L. No.104-208, Division C) provided federal standards for state drivers' licenses and birth certificates when used as identification-related documents for federal purposes. A state had two choices under this provision. It could require that each of its licenses include the licensee's Social Security number in machine-readable or visually readable form. Or the state could more minimally require that each applicant submit the applicant's Social Security number and verify the legitimacy of that number with the Social Security Administration. However, this section became subject to widespread public criticism shortly after its enactment, with opponents most frequently alleging that it could be construed as a step toward a national identification card system. Congress blocked funds to implement regulations aimed at assisting the states to adopt the Social Security number requirements, and the underlying requirement itself was subsequently repealed in § 355 of the Department of Transportation and Related Agencies Appropriations Act 2000 (Pub. L. No. 106-69). Prior to 9/11, legislation aimed at discouraging national standards for identification documents had gained bipartisan support and was thought likely to pass.

[90] Pub. L. No. 108-458 §§ 7211-7214.

[91] As mentioned previously, a bill containing only the provisions of H.R. 418 relating to drivers' licenses and personal identification cards, has also been introduced. See Driver's License Security and Modernization Act, H.R. 368, 109th Cong. (1st Sess. 2005).

[92] See Pub. L. No. 108-458, § 7212. Whether limiting the standards to federal acceptance - as opposed to direct federal prescriptions on the states - obviates federalism concerns under Supreme Court jurisprudence, remains to be seen. The Court has held that in exercising its power under the Commerce Clause, Congress may not "commandeer" the state regulatory processes by ordering states to enact or administer a federal regulatory program. See New York v United States, 505 U.S. 144 (1992). The Court has extended this principle by holding, in Printz v. United States, that Congress may not circumvent the prohibition on commandeering a state's regulatory processes "by conscripting the State's officers directly." Printz v. United States, 521 U.S. 898, 935 (1997). It may be possible to argue that, because the issuance of drivers' licenses remains a state regulatory function, the minimum issuance and verification requirements established in this bill, even if limited to federal agency acceptance, constitute an effective commandeering by Congress of the state regulatory process, or a conscription of the state and local officials who issue the licenses.

[93] Pub. L. No. 108-458, § 7212(b)(2)(D)(i)-(vii).

[94] Id. at § 7212(b)(2)(E)-(F).

[95] Id. at § 7212(b)(2)(G).

[96] Id. at § 7212(b)(2)(A)-(C).

[97] Id. at § 7212(b)(3)(B).

[98] Id. at § 7212(b)(3)(C).

[99] Pub. L. No. 108-458, § 7212(b)(3)(D)-(E).

[100] See Negotiated Rulemaking Act of 1990, Pub. L. No. 101-648, 104 Stat. 4970 (1990) (codified as amended at 5 U.S.C. §§ 581 et seq.).

[101] See Pub. L. No. 108-458, § 7212(b)(4)(A)-(B).

[102] Although H.R. 418 does not directly impose federal standards with respect to states' issuance of drivers' licenses and personal identification cards, states would nevertheless appear to need to adopt such standards and modify any conflicting laws or regulations in order for such documents to be recognized by federal agencies for official purposes

[103] For more information relating to current state laws regarding the issuance of drivers' licenses to aliens see CRS Report RL32127, Summary of State Laws on the Issuance of Driver's Licenses to Undocumented Aliens, by Allison M. Smith.

[104] According to H.R. 418, persons would only be eligible for temporary drivers' licenses or identification cards if evidence is presented that they: (1) have a valid, unexpired nonimmigrant visa or non-immigrant

visa status for entry into the United States; (2) have a pending or approved application for asylum in the United States; (3) have entered into the United States in refugee status; (4) have a pending or approved application for temporary protected status in the United States; (5) have approved deferred action status; or (6) have a pending application for adjustment of status to that of an alien lawfully admitted for permanent residence in the United States or conditional permanent resident status in the United States.

[105] In the event that a SSN is already registered to or associated with another person to which any state has issued a driver's license or identification card, the state shall resolve the discrepancy and take appropriate action.

[106] Such a provision will likely have an impact on the Constitutional analysis as indicated supra in note 92.

[107] See U.S. CONST. Art. 1 § 8, cl. 10 (stating that "[n]o state shall, without the consent of Congress, ... enter into any agreement or compact with another state, or with a foreign power...").

[108] Georgia, Kentucky, Michigan, and Wisconsin appear to be the only four states that are not currently members of the compact. See American Association of Motor Vehicle Administrators, available at [http://www.aamva.org/drivers/drv_compactsDLC.asp].

[109] These include, but are not limited to, holograms, watermarks, symbols, codes, images, or sequences. See 18 U.S.C. § 1028(d)(1) (2004).

INDEX

T

U

V

W